Print Handwriting
Workbook For Teens

Belongs to

Ango

My potential to succeed is infinite.

I am proud of my own success.

This book is organized in a progressively skill building way to help tweens, teens & young adults to develop confidence to write neatly and improve their handwriting.

With 100+ pages to write in, you will get tons of much needed repetitive practice.

This Print Handwriting workbook is divided into the following parts

Part 1: Learning the Alphabet:
　　　Trace and practice letters a-z and A-Z

Part 2: Writing two, three & four letter words and capitalization

Part 3: Writing Numbers & Number Words

Part 4: Writing Affirmations, Inspirational words & Quotes

Part 5: Writing poems by famous poets and definitions

Part 6: Writing famous speeches

You can use a pencil, light color marker or pen to trace the dotted letters and words.

Hi!

My name is Sujatha Lalgudi. I sincerely hope you find my print handwriting book to be helpful and fun.

Write to me at **sujatha.lalgudi@gmail.com** with the subject as **Teen Print** along with **your name** to get free printable practice sheets and a name tracing sheet.

If you liked this book, please do write a review on Amazon!

Your kind reviews and comments will encourage me to make more books like this.

Thank you
Sujatha Lalgudi

Part 1:
Learning Letters

Trace the letters and practice writing them in the remaining space!

Are you ready?
Let's go!

2
1
4
3

a a a a a a

a a a a a a

a a a a a

a

1 2
3

A A A A A A

A A A A A A

A A A A A

A A A A A

b b b b b b

b b b b b b

b b b b b

b b b b b

B B B B B B

B B B B B B

B B B B B B B B B B

B B B B B B B B B B B

B B B B B

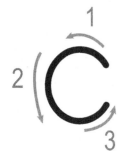

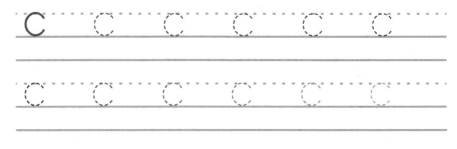

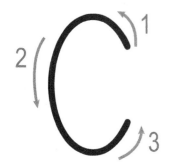

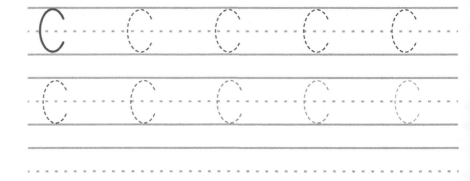

d d d d d d

d d d d d d

d

d

D D D D D D

D D D D D D

D

D

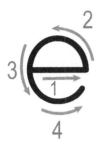

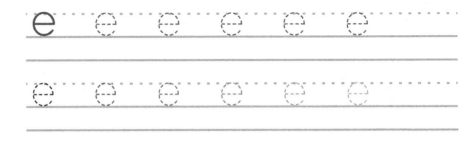

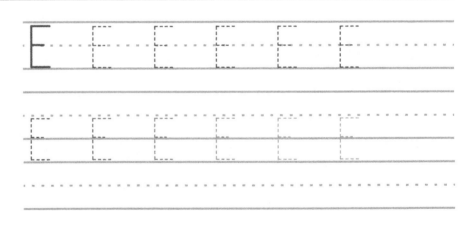

f

1
2 3

F

1
2
3

a b c d e f **g** h i j k l m n o p q r s t u v w x y z

g g g g g g g

g g g g g g

g

g

G G G G G G

G G G G G G

G

G

A B C D E F **G** H I J K L M N O P Q R S T U V W X Y Z

a b c d e f g **h** i j k l m n o p q r s t u v w x y z

h h h h h h h

h h h h h h h

h

h

H H H H H H

H H H H H H

H

H

A B C D E F G **H** I J K L M N O P Q R S T U V W X Y Z

i

•2

1 ↓

I

← 1

2 ↓

3 →

j

j j j j j j j

j j j j j j j

j

j

J

J J J J J J J

J J J J J J J

J

J

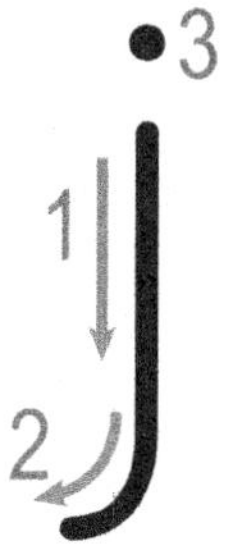

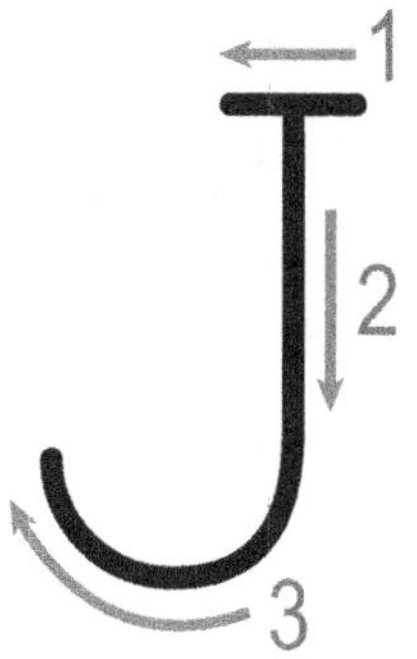

k k k k k k

k k k k k k

k

k

K K K K K K

K K K K K K

K

K

1

1
2

a b c d e f g h i j k l **m** n o p q r s t u v w x y z

m m m m m

m m m m m

m

m

M M M M M

M M M M M

M

M

A B C D E F G H I J K L **M** N O P Q R S T U V W X Y Z

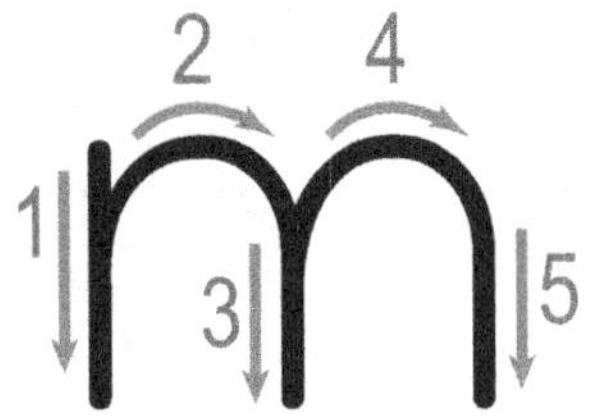

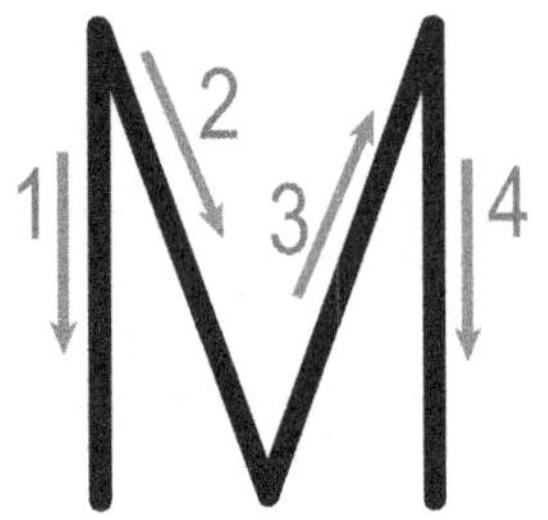

n n n n n n n
n n n n n n

2
1 n 3

n

n

N

2
1 N 3

N N N N N N
N N N N N N

N

N

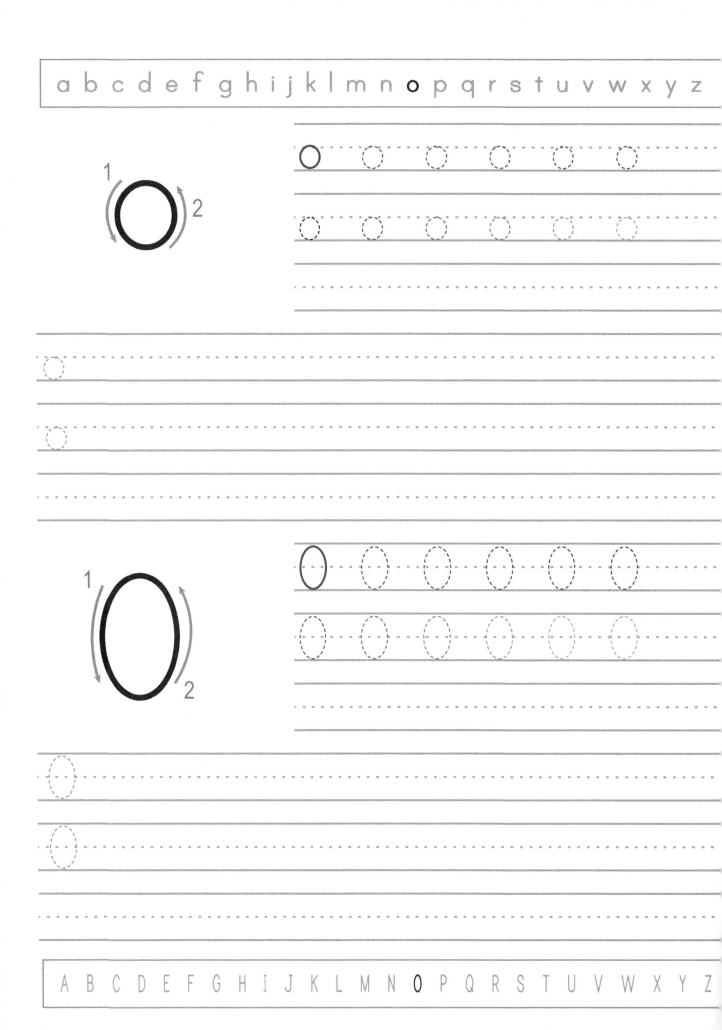

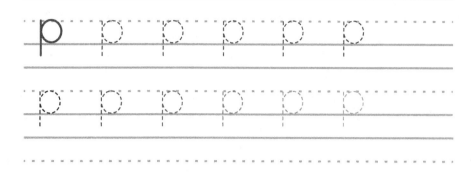

p p p p p p

p p p p p p

p

p

P P P P P P

P P P P P P

P

P

q q q q q q
q q q q q q

q

q

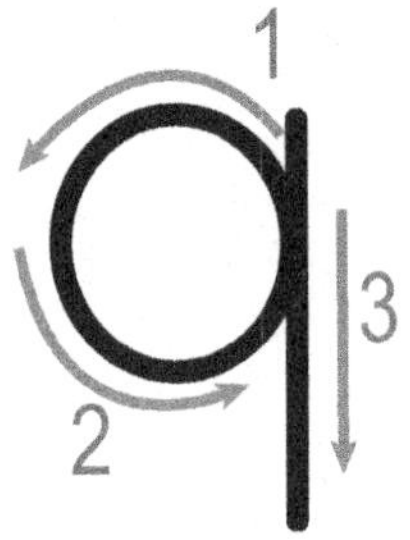

1 2 3

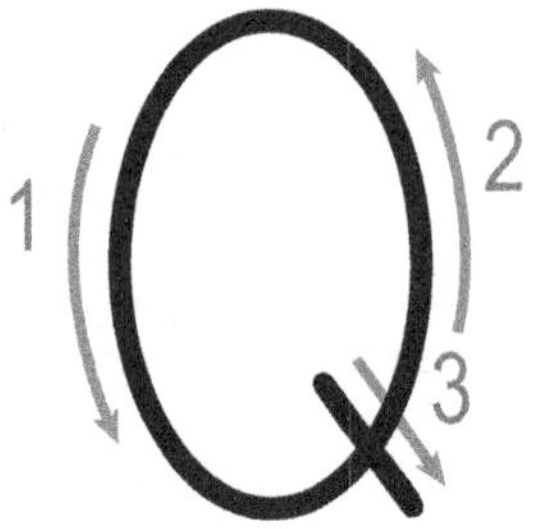

Q Q Q Q Q Q
Q Q Q Q Q Q

Q

Q

1 2 3

a b c d e f g h i j k l m n o p q **r** s t u v w x y z

r r r r r r

r r r r r r

r

r

R R R R R R

R R R R R R

R

R

A B C D E F G H I J K L M N O P Q **R** S T U V W X Y Z

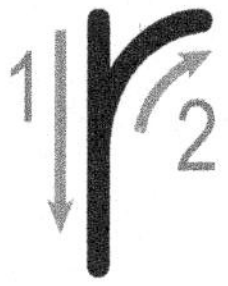

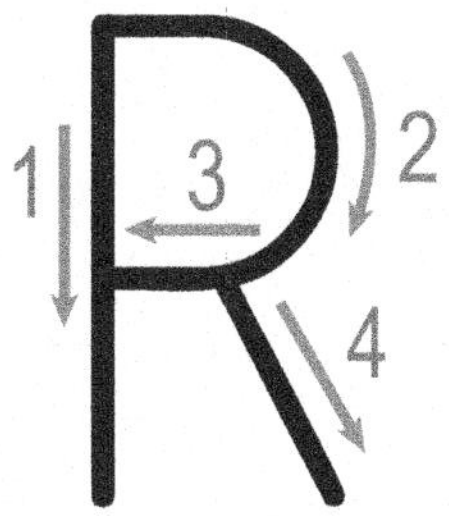

S S S S S S S

S S S S S S S

S

S

S S S S S S S

S S S S S S S

S

S

a b c d e f g h i j k l m n o p q r s t u v w x y z

u u u u u u

u u u u u u

u

u

U U U U U U

U U U U U U

U

U

A B C D E F G H I J K L M N O P Q R S T U V W X Y Z

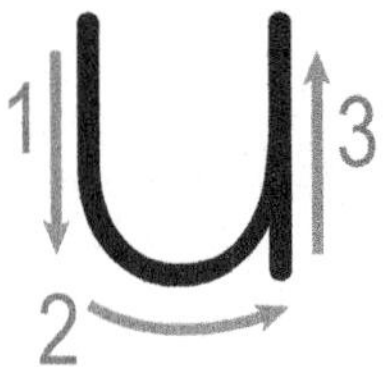

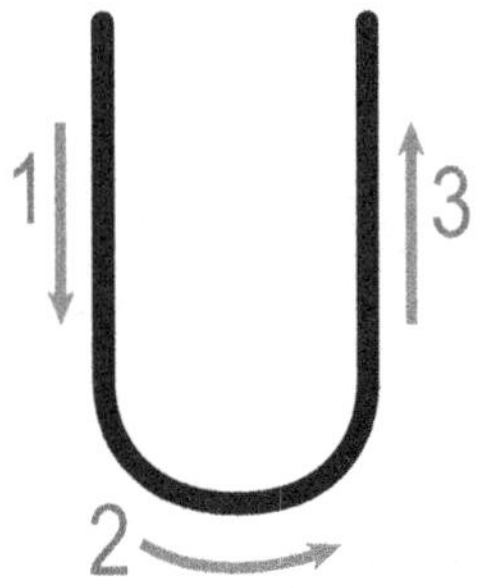

abcdefghijklmnopqrstu**v**wxyz

ABCDEFGHIJKLMNOPQRSTU**V**WXYZ

W W W W W W

W W W W W W

w

w

W W W W W

W W W W W

w

w

y

Y

a b c d e f g h i j k L m n o p q r s t u v w x y **z**

Z   Z   Z   Z   Z   Z

Z   Z   Z   Z   Z   Z

z

z

Z   Z   Z   Z   Z   Z

Z   Z   Z   Z   Z   Z

z

z

A B C D E F G H I J K L M N O P Q R S T U V W X Y **Z**

a b c d e f g h i j k l m n o p q r s t u v w x y z

a b c d e f g h i j k l m n o
p q r s t u v w x y z
a b c d e f g h i j k l m n o
p q r s t u v w x y z
a b c d e f g h i j k l m n o
p q r s t u v w x y z
a b c d e f g h i j k l m n o
p q r s t u v w x y z

A B C D E F G H I J K L M N O P Q R S T U V W X Y Z

a b c d e f g h i j k l m n o p q r s t u v w x y z

A B C D E F G H I J K L M
N O P Q R S T U V W X Y Z
A B C D E F G H I J K L M
N O P Q R S T U V W X Y Z
A B C D E F G H I J K L M
N O P Q R S T U V W X Y Z
A B C D E F G H I J K L M
N O P Q R S T U V W X Y Z

A B C D E F G H I J K L M N O P Q R S T U V W X Y Z

a b c d e f g h i j k l m n o p q r s t u v w x y z

Aa Bb Cc Dd Ee Ff Gg Hh Ii

Jj Kk Ll Mm Nn Oo Pp Qq Rr

Ss Tt Uu Vv Ww Xx Yy Zz

Aa Bb Cc Dd Ee Ff Gg Hh Ii

Jj Kk Ll Mm Nn Oo Pp Qq Rr

Ss Tt Uu Vv Ww Xx Yy Zz

Aa Bb Cc Dd Ee Ff Gg Hh Ii

Jj Kk Ll Mm Nn Oo Pp Qq Rr

Ss Tt Uu Vv Ww Xx Yy Zz

A B C D E F G H I J K L M N O P Q R S T U V W X Y Z

Part 2:
Words

Two, three, four letter words & capitalization

We will now practice writing
words using a smaller letter size.

Trace the words and practice writing
them in the remaining space!

You are
AMAZING!

an an an an an an

be be be be be be

do do do do do do

go go go go go go

hi hi hi hi hi hi

it it it it it it

lo lo lo lo lo lo

my my my my my my

no no no no no no

of of of of of of

pi pi pi pi pi pi

so so so so so so

to to to to to to

us us us us us us

we we we we we we

Practice writing your own words here:

air   air   air   air   air   air

bag   bag   bag   bag   bag   bag

car   car   car   car   car   car

did   did   did   did   did   did

eel   eel   eel   eel   eel   eel

far   far   far   far   far   far

got   got   got   got   got   got

has   has   has   has   has   has

ink ink ink ink ink ink

jet jet jet jet jet jet

key key key key key key

lid lid lid lid lid lid

mat mat mat mat mat

net net net net net net

oil oil oil oil oil oil

pro pro pro pro pro pro

rug rug rug rug rug rug

say say say say say say

tag tag tag tag tag tag

use use use use use use

van van van van van van

web web web web web

yet yet yet yet yet yet

zap zap zap zap zap zap

able able able able able

bold bold bold bold bold

crew crew crew crew crew

down down down down down

even even even even even

farm farm farm farm farm

good good good good good

hand hand hand hand hand

idle   idle   idle   idle   idle

joke   joke   joke   joke   joke

kind   kind   kind   kind   kind

list   list   list   list   list

mine   mine   mine   mine   mine

nest   nest   nest   nest   nest

oven   oven   oven   oven   oven

part   part   part   part   part

quit quit quit quit quit

roar roar roar roar roar

sand sand sand sand sand

time time time time time

used used used used used

vent vent vent vent vent

work work work work work

x ray x ray x ray x ray x ray

year year year year year

zoom zoom zoom zoom zoom

Write your own words here:

Ate Ate Ate Ate Ate

Bus Bus Bus Bus Bus

Can Can Can Can Can

Dog Dog Dog Dog Dog

Eat Eat Eat Eat Eat

Far Far Far Far Far Far

Gum Gum Gum Gum Gum

Had Had Had Had Had

Ink Ink Ink Ink Ink Ink

Jag Jag Jag Jag Jag

Kin Kin Kin Kin Kin

Lit Lit Lit Lit Lit Lit

Met Met Met Met Met

Not Not Not Not Not

Odd Odd Odd Odd Odd

Pay Pay Pay Pay Pay

Quit Quit Quit Quit Quit

Rug Rug Rug Rug Rug

Sun Sun Sun Sun Sun

Top Top Top Top Top Top

Use Use Use Use Use Use

Vest Vest Vest Vest Vest

Win Win Win Win Win

Xenon Xenon Xenon Xenon

Yak   Yak   Yak   Yak   Yak

Zoo   Zoo   Zoo   Zoo   Zoo

Write your own words here:

Part 3:
Numbers & Number Words

We will now practice writing numbers
and number words.

Trace the dotted numbers and number words,
then write them in the remaining space.
Use your best handwriting!

You are
AWESOME!

1 2 3 4 5 6 7 8 9 10

1 2 3 4 5 6 7 8 9 10

1 2 3 4 5 6 7 8 9 10

1 2 3 4 5 6 7 8 9 10

1 2 3 4 5 6 7 8 9 10

1 2 3 4 5 6 7 8 9 10

11 11 11 11 11 11 11 11 11

12 12 12 12 12 12 12 12 12

13 13 13 13 13 13 13 13

14 14 14 14 14 14 14 14

15 15 15 15 15 15 15 15

16 16 16 16 16 16 16 16

17 17 17 17 17 17 17 17

18 18 18 18 18 18 18 18

19 19 19 19 19 19 19 19

20 20 20 20 20 20 20 20

11 12 13 14 15 16 17 18 19 20

20 21 22 23 24 25 26 27 28 29

30 31 32 33 34 35 36 37 38 39

40 41 42 43 44 45 46 47 48 49

50 51 52 53 54 55 56 57 58 59

60 61 62 63 64 65 66 67 68 69

70 71 72 73 74 75 76 77 78 79

80 81 82 83 84 85 86 87 88 89

90 91 92 93 94 95 96 97 98 99

100 200 300 400 500 600 700

800 900 1000

1 — One   1 — One

2 — Two   2 — Two

3 — Three   3 — Three

4 — Four   4 — Four

5 — Five   5 — Five

6 — Six   6 — Six

7 — Seven   7 — Seven

8 — Eight   8 — Eight

9 — Nine   9 — Nine

10 — Ten   10 — Ten

One   One   One   One   One   One

Two   Two   Two   Two   Two   Two

Three   Three   Three   Three   Three

Four   Four   Four   Four   Four

Five   Five   Five   Five   Five

Six   Six   Six   Six   Six   Six

Seven   Seven   Seven   Seven

Eight   Eight   Eight   Eight   Eight

Nine   Nine   Nine   Nine   Nine

Ten   Ten   Ten   Ten   Ten   Ten

Eleven   Eleven   Eleven   Eleven

Twelve   Twelve   Twelve   Twelve

Thirteen   Thirteen   Thirteen   Thirteen

Fourteen   Fourteen   Fourteen   Fourteen

Fifteen   Fifteen   Fifteen   Fifteen

Sixteen   Sixteen   Sixteen   Sixteen

Seventeen   Seventeen   Seventeen

Eighteen   Eighteen   Eighteen

Nineteen   Nineteen   Nineteen

Twenty   Twenty   Twenty   Twenty

Part 4:
Sentences

We will now practice writing
sentences using a smaller letter size.

Trace the dotted pangrams, affirmations, quotes
and then practice writing them on your own.

You can try writing your own affirmations &
quotes on the blank sheet(s)
at the end of this part!

Use your best handwriting!

Great
Going!

How quickly daft jumping zebras vex.

Pangram: A pangram is a sentence that contains every letter of the alphabet at least once. Practice these fun lines.

Two driven jocks help fax my big quiz.

Sphinx of black quartz, judge my vow!

Fix problem quickly with galvanized jets.

The five boxing wizards jump quickly.

The quick brown fox jumps over a lazy dog.

How vexingly quick daft zebras jump!

The jay, pig, fox, zebra and my wolves quack!

Write your own Pangram here:

Today is going to be a good day.

I live each day to the fullest.

I am worthy of greatness.

My potential to succeed is infinite.

I don't need to be perfect.

Today, I will walk through my fears.

I celebrate my individuality.

I am an amazing person.

I love myself.

I have courage and confidence

I am smart, capable and valuable

I love and enjoy everything I do

I can get through anything

I set goals and I reach them

I am my own superhero

I can make a difference

I have the power to create change

I will become what I know I can be

I trust myself

I am proud of my own success

I am focused, persistent and will never quit

I respect and treat myself with kindness
and love

I take pride in the progress I make each
day

I am beautiful on the outside as I am on
the inside

"The journey of a thousand miles begins with one step." — Lao Tzu

"You must be the change you wish to see in the world." — Mahatma Gandhi

"Make each day your masterpiece." — John Wooden

"Action is the foundational key to all success." — Pablo Picasso

"We are what we repeatedly do

Excellence, then, is not an act, but a habit"

— Aristotle

"Give every day the chance to become the

most beautiful day of your life"

— Mark Twain

"Success occurs when opportunity meets

preparation." — Zig Ziglar

The difference between ordinary and
extraordinary is that little extra."
— Jimmy Johnson

"Your imagination is your preview of life's
coming attractions." — Albert Einstein

Don't wait. The time will never be just right."
— Napoleon Hill

I will go anywhere as long as it is forward."
— David Livingston

"If you can believe it," the mind can achieve
it." — Ronnie Lott

"Everything is practice." — Bill Shankley

"The harder I work, the luckier I get."
— Gary Player

"A champion is someone who gets up when
he can't." — Jack Dempsey

"Dream big and dare to fail."
— Norman Vaughan

"Begin by always expecting good things to happen." — Tom Hopkins

"Don't watch the clock; do what it does. Keep going." — Sam Levenson

"Well done is better than well said." — Benjamin Franklin

"If opportunity doesn't knock, build a door." — Milton Berle

"Your time is limited, so don't waste it

living someone else's life."

— Steve Jobs

"Your attitude, not your aptitude, will

determine your altitude."

— Zig Ziglar

"An obstacle is often a stepping stone."

— William Prescott

Courage is never to let your actions be influenced by your fears." — Arthur Koestler

Energy and persistence conquer all things" — Benjamin Franklin

Tough times never last, but tough people do." — Dr. Robert Schuller

Happiness is not something readymade. It comes from your own actions." — Dalai Lama

"Give every day the chance to become the
most beautiful day of your life."
— Mark Twain

"I am not a product of my circumstances.
I am a product of my decisions."
— Stephen Covey

"What we dwell on is who we become."
— Oprah Winfrey

"Everything is practice." — Bill Shankley

"Though no one can go back and make a
brand new start, anyone can start from now
and make a brand new ending." — Carl Bard

"Success is the sum of small efforts,
repeated day in and day out."
— Robert Collier

"Either you run the day, or the day runs you."
— Jim Rohn

"The ladder of success is best climbed
by stepping on the rungs of opportunity."
— Ayn Rand

"Enjoy the little things, for one day you may
look back and realize they were the big
things." — Robert Brault

"The only way to do great work is to love
what you do." — Steve Jobs

Sujatha Lalgudi

Part 5:
Poetry

Trace the definition of poetic forms and the poems by famous poets.
Practice writing them on your own on the blank page provided on the right handed side.

Use your best handwriting!

You are brilliant!

Definitions

SONNET - Sonnet is a poem of fourteen lines using any of a number of formal rhyme schemes having ten syllables per line.

HAIKU - Haiku is a Japanese poem of seventeen syllables, in three lines of five, seven, and five, traditionally evoking images of the natural world.

ODE - Ode is a lyric poem in the form of an address to a particular subject, often elevated in style or manner and written in varied or irregular meter.

ACROSTIC - Acrostic is a poem, word puzzle, or other composition in which certain letters in each line form word(s).

EPIC - Epic is a long poem narrating the deeds and adventures of heroic or legendary figures or the history of a nation.

Sujatha Lalgudi

Definitions

FREE VERSE: Free verse is poetry that does not rhyme or have a regular meter.

RHYME: A rhyme is a poem composed of lines that end in words or syllables with sounds that correspond with those at the the ends of other lines.

BALLAD: A ballad is a poem narrating a story in short stanzas. Traditional ballads are typically of unknown authorship, having been passed on orally from one generation to the next as part of the folk culture.

LIMERICK: A limerick is a humorous verse frequently bawdy, of three long and two short lines rhyming AABBA.

NARRATIVE: A narrative poem in literature is a poem which tells a story through verse. It has plot, characters, and setting.

The Echoing Green

— William Blake

The Sun does arise,

And make happy the skies.

The merry bells ring

To welcome the Spring.

The sky-lark and thrush,

The birds of the bush,

Sing louder around,

To the bells' cheerful sound.

While our sports shall be seen

On the Echoing Green.

Old John with white hair

Does laugh away care,

Sitting under the oak,

Among the old folk,

They laugh at our play,

The Echoing Green (Continued)

And soon they all say

Such such were the joys

When we all —girls and boys—

In our youth-time were seen,

The sky-lark and thrush,

On the Echoing Green.

Till the little ones weary

No more can be merry

The sun does descend,

And our sports have an end.

Round the laps of their mothers,

Many sisters and brothers,

Like birds in their nest

Are ready for rest,

And sport no more seen

On the darkening Green.

The Road Not Taken

~ Robert Frost

Two roads diverged in a yellow wood,

And sorry I could not travel both

And be one traveler, long I stood

And looked down one as far as I could

To where it bent in the undergrowth;

Then took the other, as just as fair,

And having perhaps the better claim,

Though as for that the passing there

Had worn them really about the same,

And both that morning equally lay

Oh, I kept the first for another day!

Yet knowing how way leads on to way,

I doubted if I should ever come back.

Sujatha Lalgudi

The Road Not Taken (Continued ...)

~ Robert Frost

I shall be telling this with a sigh

Somewhere ages and ages hence:

Two roads diverged in a wood, and I

I took the one less traveled by,

And that has made all the difference.

·· * ··

William Blake was an English poet, painter and printmaker. Blake is held in high regard by later critics for his expressiveness and creativity, and for the philosophical and mystical undercurrents within his work. He is now considered a seminal figure in the history of the poetry and visual arts of the Romantic Age.

Robert Lee Frost was an American poet. His work was initially published in England before it was published in the United States. Frost was honored frequently during his lifetime and is the only poet to receive four Pulitzer Prizes for Poetry. He was awarded the Congressional Gold Medal in 1960 for his poetic works. On July 22, 1961, Frost was named poet laureate of Vermont.

Sujatha Lalgudi

Part 6:
Famous Person

Trace the famous words by Madame Curie.

Famous Speeches

Trace the famous speeches.
Practice writing them on your own
on the blank page provided on
the right handed side.

Use your best handwriting!

Fantastic!

Madame Marie Curie (1867 - 1934) was a Polish and naturalized-French physicist and chemist who conducted pioneering research. She was the first woman to become a professor at the University of Paris in 1906, the first woman to win a Nobel prize, and the only person to win the Nobel Prize in two scientific fields. She shared the 1903 Nobel Prize in Physics with Pierre Curie and with the physicist Henri Becquerel for their pioneering work developing the theory of "radioactivity" — a term she coined. Marie won the 1911 Nobel Prize in Chemistry for her discovery of the elements polonium and radium. In addition to her Nobel Prizes, she has received numerous other honours and tributes.

Quotes by Madame Curie:

"Be less curious about people and more curious about ideas"

"Nothing in life is to be feared, it is only to be understood. Now is the time to understand more, so that we may fear less."

"It is my earnest desire that some of you should carry on this scientific work and keep for your ambition the determination to make a permanent contribution to science"

"I am among those who think that science has great beauty. A scientist in his laboratory is not only a technician: he is also a child placed before natural phenomena which impress him like a fairy tale."

We must not forget that when radium was discovered no one knew that it would prove useful in hospitals. The work was one of pure science. And this is a proof that scientific work must not be considered from the point of view of the direct usefulness of it. It must be done for itself, for the beauty of science, and then there is always the chance that a scientific discovery may become like the radium a benefit for humanity."

The Pleasure Of Books

April 6, 1933 -- Radio broadcast

William Lyon Phelps

The habit of reading is one of the greatest resources of mankind; and we enjoy reading books that belong to us much more than if they are borrowed. A borrowed book is like a guest in the house; it must be treated with punctiliousness, with a certain considerate formality. You must see that it sustains no damage; it must not suffer while under your roof. You cannot leave it carelessly, you cannot mark it, you cannot turn down the pages, you cannot use it familiarly. And then some day, although this is seldom done, you really ought to return it.

But your own books belong to you; you treat

The Pleasure Of Books (continued)

them with that affectionate intimacy that
annihilates formality. Books are for use, not
for show. you should own no book that you ar
afraid to mark up, or afraid to place on the
table, wide open and face down. A good
reason for marking favorite passages in book
is that this practice enables you to remember
more easily the significant sayings, to refer t
them quickly, and then in later years, it is like
visiting a forest where you once blazed a
trail. You have the pleasure of going over the
old ground, and recalling both the intellectua
scenery and your own earlier self.

Everyone should begin collecting a private
library in youth. the instinct of private
property, which is fundamental in human

Sujatha Lalgudi

The Pleasure Of Books (continued ...)
beings, can here be cultivated with every
advantage and no evils. One should have
one's own bookshelves, which should not have
doors, glass windows, or keys; they should be
free and accessible to the hand as well as
to the eye. The best of mural decorations is
books; they are more varied in color and
appearance than any wallpaper, they are
more attractive in design, and they have the
prime advantage of being separate
personalities, so that if you sit alone in the
room in the firelight, you are surrounded with
intimate friends. The knowledge that they are
there in plain view is both stimulating and
refreshing. You do not have to read them all.
Most of my indoor life is spent in a room
containing six thousand books, and I have a

The Pleasure Of Books (continued...)

stock answer to the invariable question that
comes from strangers: "Have you read all of
these books?"
"Some of them twice."
This reply is both true and unexpected.

There are of course no friends like living,
breathing, corporeal men and women; my
devotion to reading has never made me a
recluse. How could it? Books are of the
people, by the people, for the people.
Literature is the immortal part of history; it is
the best and most enduring part of
personality. But book-friends have this
advantage over living friends: you can enjoy
the most truly aristocratic society in the
world whenever you want it. The great dead

Sujatha Lalgudi

The Pleasure Of Books (continued ...)

are beyond our physical reach, and the great
living are usually almost as inaccessible. As
for our personal friends and acquaintances,
we cannot always see them. Perchance they
are asleep, or away on a journey. But in a
private library, you can at any moment
converse with Socrates or Shakespeare or
Carlyle or Dumas or Dickens or Shaw or
Barrie or Galsworthy. And there is no doubt
that in these books you see these men at
their best. They wrote for you. They "laid
themselves out," they did their ultimate best
to entertain you, to make a favorable
impression. You are necessary to them as an
audience is to an actor, only instead of
seeing them masked, you look into their
innermost heart of heart.

© Sujatha Lalgudi

Farewell To Baseball

July 4, 1939 - Yankee Stadium, New York

Lou Gehrig

Fans, for the past two weeks you have
been reading about a bad break I got.
Yet today I consider myself the luckiest man
on the face of the earth.

I have been in ballparks for seventeen years
and have never received anything but
kindness and encouragement from you fans.
Look at these grand men. Which of you
wouldn't consider it the highlight of his
career just to associate with them for even
one day?

Sure I'm lucky.

Who wouldn't consider it an honor to have

Sujatha Lalgudi

Farewell To Baseball (continued ...)
known Jacob Ruppert? Also, the builder of
baseball's greatest empire, Ed Barrow?
To have spent six years with that wonderful
little fellow, Miller Huggins? Then to have
spent the next nine years with that
outstanding leader, that smart student of
psychology, the best manager in baseball
today, Joe McCarthy?
Sure I'm lucky

When the New York Giants, a team you would
give your right arm to beat, and vice versa,
sends you a gift — that's something. When
everybody down to the groundskeepers
and those boys in white coats remember you
with trophies — that's something

Farewell To Baseball (continued ...)

When you have a wonderful mother-in-law who takes sides with you in squabbles with her own daughter — that's something. When you have a father and a mother who work all their lives so you can have an education and build your body — it's a blessing. When you have a wife who has been a tower of strength and shown more courage than you dreamed existed — that's the finest I know.

So I close in saying that I might have been given a bad break, but I've got an awful lot to live for.

Sujatha Lalgudi

William Lyon Phelps was an American
educator, literary critic and author. He serve
as a professor of English at Yale University
He was a scholar and critic who did much t
popularize the teaching of contemporary
literature. He was a popular lecturer and his
literary essays brought him an audience
estimated in the millions   —*—

Henry Louis Gehrig was an American
professional baseball first baseman who
played 17 seasons in Major League Baseba
for the New York Yankees. He was renowne
for his prowess as a hitter and for his
durability, which earned him his nickname
"The Iron Horse". He still has the highest rati
of runs scored plus runs batted in per 100
plate appearances and was elected to the
Baseball Hall of Fame

CONGRATULATIONS!
You are a
CHAMPION!

Celebrate your Success!

Share the Joy!

Feel Great Everyday!

GRATITUDE JOURNAL

Invest
Few Minutes a Day
to develop thankfulness,
mindfulness and positivity

90 Days of daily practice

ISBN: 1777421136

Get it
Today

Hi!

Write to me at **sujatha.lalgudi@gmail.com**
with the subject as **Teen Print**
along with your name to get free printable
practice sheets.

Thank you
Sujatha Lalgudi

Congratulations

Writing Super Star
Awarded to

_____

For _____

Date _____   **Signed** _____

Made in the USA
Las Vegas, NV
07 September 2022

54829038R10063